Garsten shed, at the original northern terminus of the *Steyrtalbahn*, is the location of this scene featuring two U Class locomotives, nos 298.53 and 298.25, being prepared for service on 6th July 1976. The engine shed is as equally attractive as the locomotives.

*B Benn*

## Setting the Scene

During the 19th Century the Austro-Hungarian Empire, which occupied much of Eastern Europe, was at the forefront of railway development during that expansive period. Having completed the nucleus of its main line network, the *Lokalbahn* law of 1887 allowed the development of minor routes of both standard and narrow gauge throughout the Empire. Following its evident success in Bosnia where it was introduced in 1879, the gauge chosen for the narrow gauge lines was 760mm, which quickly became known as the *Bosnian gauge*. For strategic reasons, the Austrian military insisted that all narrow gauge railways throughout the Empire were 760mm gauge to allow the easy transfer of locomotives and rolling stock between the many isolated systems in time of war. This was of particular importance in its politically volatile regions in the Balkans. Many of the narrow gauge lines were to be operated by the Imperial-Royal Austrian State Railways (kkStB) whilst others were instigated by regional government backed concerns such as the Lower Austrian Provincial Railways (NÖLB) and *Steiermärkische Landesbahnen* (StLB). In addition there were numerous independent operations such as the *Steyrtalbahn*, the *Salzkammergut-Lokalbahn* (SKGLB) and the *Zillertalbahn* (ZB). Following the turmoil of the Great War and the ultimate collapse of the Austro-Hungarian Empire, the kkStB and NÖLB were both incorporated into Federal Railways Austria (BBÖ) in 1921. After the German annexation of Austria in 1938, the BBÖ was absorbed into the German State Railways (DRB) and the narrow gauge locomotives were re-numbered into the DRB 99.xxxx series. The former BBÖ eventually re-emerged as *Österreichische Bundesbahnen* (ÖBB) in 1947. The principal lines to retain their independence after 1947 were the StLB, SKGLB and ZB.

A sharp rise in import charges on machinery acquired from outside the Empire imposed in the late 1870s led the well established Bavarian company *Lokomotivfabrik Krauss*, which had been founded by Georg Krauss at Munich in 1866, to open a factory at Linz in 1880. *Lokomotivfabrik Krauss, Linz* was destined to construct the majority of narrow gauge locomotives supplied for use in Austria between 1888 and 1930. To cater for the needs of the many contrasting 760mm gauge railways, a range of sturdy locomotives was developed which incorporated many standardised components and were to see service throughout the Austro-Hungarian Empire, although after 1919 Austria was to become their principal field of operation. Compared to the 600mm and 750mm gauge locomotives built at Munich, which were usually small machines of either 0-4-0T and 0-6-0T configuration, those constructed at Linz tended to be larger and more powerful engines designed for heavy haulage of both passenger and freight trains. Both the Linz and Munich works also built many larger locomotives of metre and standard gauges, including rack and pinion designs. In 1930 following the merger of Krauss (Munich) and Maffei, henceforth known as Krauss-Maffei, the Linz factory was closed and the goodwill transferred to *Wiener Lokomotivfabrik AG, Floridsdorf*, based at Vienna.

The oldest surviving 760mm gauge locomotive to have been constructed at Linz is *Steyrtalbahn* no.2 SIERNING, which was delivered in 1888. This view shows the characteristic long smokebox that was fitted to the original machines. Renumbered 298.102 by ÖBB, the venerable 0-6-2T was recorded at Grünburg on 14th June 2015. The water tanks were increased in capacity during the ÖBB era.

*K Strickland*

During the course of a journey from Steyr to Grünburg, no.2 was seen passing the intermediate station at Pergern on the same day in June 2015.

*K Strickland*

## Early Six Coupled Tank Locomotives

The first railway to be constructed following the legislation of 1887 was the *Steyrtalbahn*, a 40km long line to the south of Linz. Between 1888 and 1891 the Linz works supplied five 0-6-2Ts followed by a later example in 1914. Known as *Steyrtalbahn Loks*, the initial five were fitted with an unusually long smokebox which extended well beyond the chimney line. During the same period five more locomotives of the same design were supplied to the SKGLB and another three to the Mori-Arco-Riva del Garda line in the South Tyrol. These powerful locomotives set the bench mark for the later machines to emerge from Linz. Fitted with 800mm driving wheels, 290 x 400mm cylinders, 40.15 sq.metres of heating surface, 0.80 sq.metres of grate area and a weight of 23 tonnes they were a formidable design for such a small gauge with a maximum working speed of 40km/h. The later examples supplied between 1891 and 1906 (SKGLB) and 1914 (Steyr) were fitted with conventional smokeboxes and a slightly larger boiler capacity, some of the older machines being modified in a similar fashion during the early years of the 20th Century. After the *Steyrtalbahn* was absorbed by the BBÖ and ultimately the ÖBB, the surviving examples on the line became members of the class 298.1xx series after 1947. Following the closure of the SKGLB in 1957, three were sold to the StLB for use on the Weiz to Birkfeld line where they became unofficially known as the "S Class". These have all survived into preservation with Club 760 at Frojach (S 7, S 11 and S 12) whilst the SKGLB museum at Mondsee houses SKGLB nos 4 and 9, plus no.5 repatriated from Bosnia where it had worked since 1917. Three of the original Steyr based locomotives have also survived, two on their original line at Grünburg (298.102 and 298.106) and one at Kienberg-Gaming (298.104). One of the Mori-Arco-Riva locomotives now works at Omaha Zoo in the USA, following many years service in Romania.

Between 1898 and 1902 a smaller version of the design known as the T Class (later ÖBB 198 series) was introduced, five being supplied to the two lines in Carinthia, whilst four other examples saw industrial service in Bosnia. These were fitted with 640mm driving wheels, 260 x 300mm cylinders, 26.9 sq.metres of heating surface, 0.60 sq.metres of grate area and weighed 17 tonnes. Although providing long service, particularly on the *Gurktalbahn*, they were allocated to lighter duties following the introduction of larger locomotives. One of the Bosnian locomotives has survived, being preserved on a plinth at Teslić. In 1893 three 0-6-0T locomotives were supplied to the StLB for use on the Kapfenburg to Au-Seewiesen line and a further four in 1896 to the kkStB for use on the Zell am See to Krimml line. Known as the Z Class, these 19 tonne locomotives had similar principal dimensions to the T Class machines, one of the StLB examples having survived into preservation with Club 760.

Another scene on the same occasion shows the vintage 0-6-2T polluting the atmosphere with a pre-arranged "smoke effect", a short time after the previous view was recorded.

*K Strickland*

The last of the original Steyrtalbahn Loks was delivered from Linz in 1914. No.6 (later 298.106) and named "Klaus" differed from its elder sisters in being fitted with full length tanks, similar to the U Class design. Following an extensive restoration, the fully refurbished locomotive re-entered service during 2004 and was recorded at Grünburg in October of that year.

*K Strickland*

The first 0-6-2T supplied to the SKGLB in 1890, no.3 presents a superb sight as it hauls a Salzburg bound train near Billroth in September 1956. By that period the locomotive had received a later boiler with a shorter smoke-box and a stovepipe chimney, replacing the more shapely original design.

*P Hay*

Following the closure of the SKGLB in 1957, some of the locomotives were sold to the StLB for use on the Weiz to Birkfeld line. Re-numbered S 12 by its new owners, the 1906 built 0-6-2T was resting between shunting operations at Birkfeld when it was recorded on 10th September 1958.
*D Trevor Rowe*

The last surviving Z Class 0-6-0T, StLB no.6 was viewed at Kapfenberg on 9th September 1958. Note the improvised extended coal bunker, which obviously restricted the fireman's forward vision!

*D Trevor Rowe*

One of the ubiquitous U Class 0-6-2Ts, no.298.53 was raising steam at Garsten, the original northern terminus of the *Steyrtalbahn*, when it was photographed on 5th September 1958. This is one of the locomotives that are still based on this attractive railway, which is now a successful tourist operation.

*D Trevor Rowe*

# The Ubiquitous U Class

1894 saw the introduction of the first of the U Class locomotives, which were to become synonymous with the Austrian narrow gauge lines. A total of 61 was constructed until the final example emerged from Linz in 1922. The U Class shared the same wheel and cylinder dimensions as the original Steyr machines, but had larger boilers with 46.3 sq.metres of heating surface,1.00 sq.metre grates and a weight of 24 tonnes. Increased water capacity was provided by full length tanks, which extended to the front of the smokebox. Some of the later versions were fitted with rear coal bunkers in addition to the original arrangement atop the tanks on the firemans side, this version being one tonne heavier. For working in areas of greater fire risk, many were fitted with Kobel spark arrestors, those typically Central European embellishments that look like large flower pots on top of the chimneys. Although a Krauss design, some of the U Class locomotives were erected by other manufacturers. Three were built at Floridsdorf in 1900, two by StEG at Vienna in 1902 and four at Wiener Neustadt in 1908. Supplied to many 760mm gauge lines throughout the former Empire, some remained in Central Europe following WW1 although the majority continued to work in Austria. After the formation of ÖBB in 1947, all the state owned U Class locomotives were renumbered in the 298 series. A great number have been preserved in working order with many more plinthed and mounted throughout Austria, Slovenia, the Czech Republic, Slovakia and Germany. The principal locations of the preserved examples are Bezau

An immaculate 0-6-2T no. U 40 arrives at Unzmarkt, where a connection is made with the Semmering line of the ÖBB, hauling a *Murtalbahn* train from Mauterndorf on 13th September 1958. This was one of five U Class locomotives that were built at Wiener Neustadt in 1908.

*D Trevor Rowe*

(*Wälderbähnle* 298.24 and 25), Jenbach (*Zillertalbahn* ZB1 and ZB2), Grünburg (*Steyrtalbahn* 298.52 and 53), Kienberg-Gaming (*Ybbstalbahn* 298.51), Weiz–Birkfeld (U 7, U 8 and U 44), Murau (U 11, U 40 and U 43), Obergrafendorf (298.54) and Stainz (298.56 – on loan from Club 760), in addition to Jindřichův Hradec in the Czech Republic (U37002 and U37008).

Fitted with a characteristic Kobel spark arrester chimney, no.U37002 was viewed whilst in service on the tourist railway at Jindřichův Hradec in the Czech Republic during October 2004.

*K Strickland*

U Class 0-6-2T no. 298.51 was viewed crossing the River Steyr in a very scenic location near Grünburg on 10th June 1979. Scenes like this were once an everyday occurrence throughout Austria.

*J F Organ collection*

U Class 0-6-2T no.298.53 was photographed departing from Grünburg, whilst hauling a freight train from Garsten to Klaus on 7th July 1976. The River Steyr is seen to the right of the photograph.

*B Benn*

One of the original pair of locomotives supplied to the *Zillertalbahn* in 1900, U Class no.2 ZILLERTAL was seen raising steam outside the running shed at Jenbach depot in September 1987.

*G Brown*

## Early Compound and Superheated U Class Variants

Between 1902 and 1905 a compound version known as the Uv (v = Verbund) Class was produced. These had cylinders of 320/500 x 400mm together with a larger boiler with 57.8 sq.metres of heating surface, 1.03 sq.metre grates and weighed 26 tonnes. Three were supplied to NÖLB based at St. Pölten and Gmünd, which ultimately became the 298.2xx series, with another supplied to the *Zillertalbahn*. Although similar in appearance to the simple expansion U Class locomotives, the compounds were distinguished by their different diameter cylinders with the larger low pressure version on the left hand side. All four examples have survived at Kienberg-Gaming (298.205), Obergrafendorf (298.207) and Jenbach (ZB3) plus one plinthed at Langschlag (298.206).

The Uv Class were not the first compound locomotives built at Linz. They had been preceded in 1896 by three 0-6-4Ts known as the Yv Class (later 598 Class) which were supplied to kkStB for their *Ybbstalbahn*. Fitted with 310/450 x 400 cylinders, 61.4 sq.metres heating surface, 1.03 sq.metre grates and a weight of 26.5 tonnes, they proved their worth on the line with its steep gradients at the eastern end. All three have been preserved, two on their native line (598.02 and 598.03) and another plinthed at Eichgraben near Vienna (598.01).

Another variation of the U Class was a sole superheated version supplied to NÖLB in 1905. Fitted with 340 x 400mm cylinders and piston valves, 44.6 sq.metres of heating surface and 1.03 sq.metre grates, this 26.5 tonne locomotive was used for evaluation on a number of lines following its initial allocation to St.Pölten. This was to remain the only example of a superheated version of the 0-6-2T design until some superheated locomotives of a later type were introduced in 1928. Originally numbered Uh 1 (h = Heißdampf), it was renumbered Bh 1 by the BBÖ in 1928 following the introduction of the later machines. Ultimately it became 398.01 after 1947 when it was in ÖBB service before being sold to the StLB in 1973, after which it reverted to Bh 1. This prototype locomotive is still in service hauling tourist trains on the *Murtalbahn* section of the StLB from its base at Murau.

In addition to the plethora of six coupled locomotives produced during the late 19th and early 20th centuries, Linz works also constructed a small number of 0-4-0Ts which were basically designs emanating from Krauss at Munich. Two were supplied to the SKGLB in 1890 whilst a further four went to the StLB in 1892. All were used for light duties, which they continued to perform until the last examples were withdrawn in 1953 at Salzburg and Stainz in 1969. This last example of the small StLB locomotives was rebuilt with a superheater in 1974 and has been preserved by Club 760, based at Frojach on the *Murtalbahn*. The *Zillertalbahn* took delivery of a compound 2-4-0T from Linz in 1905, which was based on an earlier Munich simple expansion design of 1885. The small ZB locomotive was employed on shunting duties until its withdrawal in 1958.

Compound Uv Class no.298.205 was recorded whilst arriving at Kienberg-Gaming, the eastern terminus of the *Ybbstalbahn* on 6th September 1958. This locomotive currently operates on the preserved mountainous section of the line.

*D Trevor Rowe*

The large diameter low pressure cylinder is clearly visible in this view of TIROL, the *Zillertalbahn* Uv Class no.3. The locomotive was running round the carriages at the upper terminus at Mayrhofen on 4th September 1990.

*J F Organ*

The same locomotive was recorded later during the same day alongside the coal stage at Jenbach, prior to an afternoon trip along the valley to Mayrhofen.

*J F Organ*

The *Zillertalbahn's* Uv Class no.3 was viewed whilst being prepared to depart from Jenbach, with one of the daily steam hauled excursions to Mayrhofen that operate on this busy railway, in September 1993.

*G Brown*

A very heavily loaded train was preparing to depart from Jenbach bound for Mayrhofen, double headed by Uv Class no.3 and the larger Uh Class no.5. Trains of this length are quite common during the peak season on the *Zillertalbahn*, such as this one photographed on 13th August 1992.

B Benn

The ZB's Uv Class no.3 was witnessed as it hauled a Mayrhofen bound train near Kaltenbach on 12th August 1992. This section of the Zillertal line was doubled in 2008 in order to cope with the intensive services operated on the railway, a combination of commuter, freight and steam hauled tourist trains.

*Miss S Benn*

Following the closure of the main Ybbstalbahn route by ÖBB after severe flood damage in 2010, only the tourist "museum" line on the mountainous eastern section of the system remains in operation. Prior to the devastation, no. Yv 2 was recorded hauling an excursion from Waidhofen to Lunz-am-See along the now closed section on 1st August 1993.

*Miss S Benn*

Yv Class compound 0-6-4T no.Yv 2 (formerly 598.02) was viewed crossing a minor road near Großhollenstein whilst hauling a charter train on the *Ybbstalbahn*. The three Yv Class locomotives were synonymous with the *Ybbstalbahn* and all have survived into preservation. Note the attractive green livery carried by this locomotive in its preserved condition.

*S Benn*

The attractive preserved no. Yv 2 was hauling another photo-charter mixed train when it was viewed on the now closed western section of the *Ybbstalbahn* during October 2004.

*K Strickland*

The prototype superheated Uh Class 0-6-2T with piston valve cylinders, no.Bh1 (formerly 398.01) now operates tourist trains on the StLB *Murtalbahn*. The unique locomotive is based at Murau where it was recorded outside the depot on 10th August 2011.

*G Jones*

The piston valve cylinders of no.Bh 1 are clearly visible in this view of the immaculate locomotive outside the depot at Murau on the same occasion.

*G Jones*

## The Spanish Connection

Spain once had a number of attractive 750mm gauge railways in addition to its many metre gauge lines. Two of the best known were the San Feliu to Gerona line, north of Barcelona, and the Castellon to Onda system further south. In 1890 both lines each took delivery of four 0-6-2Ts from Krauss, with two more to San Feliu in 1893 and 1905. The Castellon examples were compounds with the remainder being simple expansion.

Although ordered from Munich via the Krauss agents in Barcelona, these locomotives were most probably sub-contracted to Linz for construction. Not only do they bear a close resemblance to the second batch of SKGLB machines, they also had consecutive works numbers to the Austrian 0-6-2Ts of the same period. To confuse matters even more, the works plates of the Spanish locomotives state both Munich and Linz as their source of manufacture, normally only the works concerned would be indicated on the plates.

On the San Feliu to Gerona line in Eastern Spain, SFG 0-6-2T no.1 was recorded at Gerona prior to departure with a mixed train on 20th March 1960.
*L G Marshall*

When the Castellon line was closed in 1963, two of the compound 0-6-2Ts were transferred to San Feliu until that splendid railway also succumbed in 1969. Four of the locomotives have survived on plinths at San Feliu, Llagostera and two at Gerona, including one of the compound variants. Another compound is also displayed on a plinth at Borriana near Castellon. The exhibit at Llagostera is in a private collection and resides under an awning in the garden of its owners premises!

Sister locomotive SFG no.6 was photographed as it ran around its carriages at Gerona on the same occasion in 1960.

*L G Marshall*

One of the compound variants of the Krauss design originally supplied to the Castellon to Onda line in 1890, no.7 was recorded at Grao de Castellon depot on 16th October 1957.

*L G Marshall*

The final compound version supplied in 1890, no.8 was witnessed as it was about to depart from the principal station at Castellon with a train bound for Onda on the same day in October 1957.

*L G Marshall*

As a reminder of happier days, SFG no.1 now resides on a plinth situated near the esplanade at San Feliu. The delightful exhibit was photographed in its attractive setting during August 1997.

*J F Organ*

## Bosnian Superpower

As recorded above, initial trials with compounds and superheating were carried out in a fairly limited way at Linz during the first years of the 20th century. However the extensive 760mm gauge network in Bosnia, required larger locomotives for its heavy passenger and freight trains.

Between 1903 and 1907 a total of 24 compound 0-8-2 tender locomotives were constructed at Linz for the Bosnian system, plus a further five built at Budapest. Equipped with 900mm driving wheels, 370/550 x 450mm cylinders, 112 sq.metre heating surface and weighing 36 tonnes (less tenders), these 83 Class locomotives were an instant success. In 1909 a superheated simple expansion version was introduced, which was even more successful. The principal dimensions were the same as the compounds, 430 x 450mm cylinders with piston valves and 88.21 sq.metre heating surface being the principal changes. Ultimately the superheated 83 Class comprised a total of 153 locomotives of which 43 were built at Linz. The remaining examples were constructed by Budapest, by Jung (24) or by Đuro Đaković in Yugoslavia, the latter concern continuing production of the 83 Class 0-8-2s until 1949. Although a large number have survived, mainly the Jung-built and the later ĐĐ machines, only one of the Linz built examples has survived in active service, no.83-076 which currently works in Austria at the *Zillertalbahn* as their no.ZB4 and is on a long term loan from Club 760 at Frojach.

For express passenger services in Bosnia, Krauss designed the 73 Class superheated 2-6-2 tender locomotives.

No.83-066, an 83 Class 0-8-2, was viewed at the head of a mixed train at Drežnica on the heavily graded Bosnian system on 25th August 1961.

*D Trevor Rowe*

One of the original compound 0-8-2s, no.83-138 was viewed to the right of one of the Budapest built 2-8-2s no.85-032 at Hum on 26th August 1961.

*D Trevor Rowe*

Fitted with 1100 mm driving wheels, 370 x 450 mm piston valve cylinders, 77.35 sq.metre heating surface and a weight of 30.5 tonnes (minus tender), these were the greyhounds of the network. 15 were supplied from Linz in 1907 with a further eight from Budapest in 1913. One of the latter, no.73-019 now works in Austria and is based at Zell-am-See. Two other members of the class, including a Linz built machine, have been preserved in Bosnia.

The 83 and 73 Class locomotives were to become synonymous with the 760mm gauge railways in Yugoslavia along with the later 85 Class 2-8-2 machines designed and built in Budapest, and later also built in Yugoslavia. These three types ultimately replaced a vast assortment of earlier mainly Munich designed locomotives including many semi-articulated radial designs on the Klose principal, most of which were constructed at Linz though in line with the quota system introduced in 1897, some were also built in Hungary at the Budapest and Arad works.

83-066 was viewed at the head of a passenger train at Ostrožac on 25th August 1961. This was one of the locomotives built in Germany by Jung in 1923.

*D Trevor Rowe*

Budapest built locomotive no.83-024 was receiving some attention from a member of the crew when it was recorded at Lašva, at the head of a lengthy freight train on 24th August 1961.

*D Trevor Rowe*

With its large spark arresting chimney very prominent in this view, another Budapest example no.83-165 was seen hauling another long freight train at Tarčin on 25th August 1961.

*D Trevor Rowe*

Bosnian superpower in all its glory. Linz 0-8-2 no.83-126 and 2-8-2 no.85-032 were witnessed as they departed from Dubrovnik whilst heading for the mountains of the hinterland with a passenger train on 26th August 1961.

*D Trevor Rowe*

The last surviving Linz built 83 Class 0-8-2 in working order is now based on the *Zillertalbahn* as no.ZB4, on long term loan from its owners Club 760. Formerly no.83-076 built in 1909, it was seen at Jenbach depot alongside various diesel powered locomotives during June 1996.

*G Brown*

One of the sprightly 73 Class 2-6-2s of the Bosnian system, Budapest built no.73-018 was hauling a mixed train at Lašva during August 1961. Sister locomotive no. 73-019 is the sole working example of these fine machines and is now based in Austria on the Zell-am-See to Krimml line.

*D Trevor Rowe*

The impressive large 83 Class locomotive was working a seasonal train from Jenbach to Mayrhofen, when it was recorded on Christmas Day 2002.

*K Strickland*

## The Engerths

The success of these superheated locomotives in Bosnia led to the Linz works producing another eight coupled design for use on the NÖLB *Mariazellerbahn*. These were the Mh Class superheated 0-8+4 Engerths with their close fitted tenders, the first of which were four supplied in 1906 followed by another two in 1908. The principal dimensions were similar to the 83 Class, the main difference being 410 x 450mm piston valve cylinders, 78.8 sq.metres of heating surface and 1.60 sq.metres grate area. The total weight including tender was 45.08 tonnes. The advantage of the Engerth design, with the tender permanently coupled to the locomotive through sliding arms alongside the firebox was that it offered smoother running than a conventional 0-8-0.

In 1907 two compound versions of the Engerth machines, known as the Mv Class were constructed for comparison. These had 370/550 x 450mm cylinders and 95.04 sq.metre heating surface. Following the electrification of the Mariazellerbahn in 1911, nos Mh 1 - Mh 6 led a somewhat peripatetic existence but gradually gravitated towards Gmünd near the Czech border where they spent much of their subsequent working lives, becoming nos 399.01 - 399.06 after 1947. Mv 1 and Mv 2 were based at Obergrafendorf for working freight trains on the line to Gresten, being numbered 299.01 and 299.02 in 1947. All of the Mh Class have survived at Gmünd (399.01, 02 and 04), Zell-am-See (Mh 3), Obergrafendorf (Mh 6) and Grünburg (399.05), unlike the two Mvs which were withdrawn during the early 1960s (the frames of one were used as a

basis for a snowplough). During 1911 three conventional 0-8-2T variants of the Mh Class machines, known as the P Class, were supplied to the Trieste-Parenzo railway which was to become embraced by both Italy and Slovenia following WW1.

No. 399.01 hauls a tourist train alongside the river at Neukirchen on 11th August 1992. This part of the Krimml line suffered serious flood damage in 2005 and was subsequently rebuilt on a new alignment by SLB. Sister locomotive no.399.03, restored as no.Mh 3, is now based on the line.

*Miss S Benn*

The purposeful appearance of the Mh Class 0-8+4 Engerth design is clearly shown in this view of no.399.01 at Alt Nagelberg with a passenger train on the northern section of the *Waldviertelbahn* near Gmünd in May 1983.
*R Todt / BVA*

The close coupled tender of Mh Class 0-8+4 no.399.01 is clearly shown in this view of the Engerth locomotive at Zell-am-See in September 1990.

*J F Organ*

Running tender first, Mh Class no.399.06 was recorded departing from Wieselburg with a passenger train bound for Gresten on 6th September 1958. A connection with the standard gauge branch from Kienberg-Gaming was made at this station.

*D Trevor Rowe*

Mh Class no.399.04 was working between Gmünd and Groß Gerungs on the *Waldviertelbahn* when it was recorded hauling a passenger train on the steeply graded line during October 2004.

*K Strickland*

Engerth 0-8+4 no.399.02 was seen at Gmünd depot prior to a journey to Groß Gerungs with a service train in September 1995. Gmünd was the "last bastion of steam" in Austria for regular service trains.

*K Strickland*

The distinctive lines of the K Class 0-8-0WT were shown to advantage in this view of no. R410.001 at Chiusa (formerly Klausen) in June 1959. *R.Todt / BVA*

## Italian Interlude

A reversion to a simple expansion saturated design occurred in 1916 when Linz supplied seven 0-8-0WTs to the Austrian Army for a 32.6 km long military railway situated in the Dolomite region of the South Tyrol. Known as the K Class, this well tank design incorporated 750mm driving wheels, 325 x 350mm cylinders, 48.14 sq.metres of heating surface, 1.00 sq.metre grates and a weight of 22 tonnes. Following the end of WW1 and South Tyrol becoming part of Italy, the scenic line running from Chiusa (formerly Klausen) to Plan was transferred to the Italian State Railways (FS). The seven locomotives continued to operate the service, apart from two sent to the Balkans during WW2, until it was closed in 1960. One of the 0-8-0WTs

A detailed view of no. R410.001 was obtained at Plan on the same date in 1959. Despite being fitted with well-tanks, the design of the locomotive has all the hallmarks of the Krauss (Linz) works. *R.Todt / BVA*

has survived on a plinth at Plan.

In 1925 five 0-10-0WT variants of the K Class were supplied from the Linz works for use on the Krivaja forestry railway in Bosnia where they earned the nickname of "Bimba" locomotives. During the same period the SKGLB took delivery of a compound 0-8-0T from Linz, closely based on the Cv Class. This sole example was mainly employed hauling freight trains between Salzburg and Bad Ischl until the untimely closure of the SKGLB in 1957.

The Alpine village of S.Christina was the location for this view of no. R410.001 as it stopped to replenish its water supply, during the course of a journey from Chuisa to Plan on the same date. *R.Todt / BVA*

## The Final Locomotives from Linz

Following the turmoil of WW1 and the break up of the Austro-Hungarian Empire, the Krauss works at Linz entered a period of consolidation during which time they constructed some Munich designed industrial 0-4-0Ts and 0-6-0Ts plus the final examples of their pre-war designs. The latter included the last U Class locomotive in 1922 (no.U 44) and the above mentioned SKGLB 0-8-0T in 1923.

## Heavy Freight Locomotives

1924 saw the start of what could be described as the "final fling" from Linz. This was the first of three superheated Kh Class 0-10-0Ts which was supplied to the Kühnsdorf line in Carinthia. Two more were supplied to the StLB in 1926 and 1930 where they were normally employed on freight duties. In order to traverse tight radius curves, these locomotives were fitted with inside frames for the four leading axles whilst the fifth axle was within splayed outside frames with liberal provision for lateral movement provided by the *Klien Lindner* system of articulation. The principal dimensions of the Kh Class were 800mm wheels, 400 x 400mm cylinders, 50.36 sq.metre heating surface, 1.21 sq.metre grates and a weight of 33.3 tonnes. The final member of the class, Kh 111, was fitted with Caprotti valve gear in place of the piston valves of 499.01 and Kh 101. The original machine was fitted with a Giesl Ejector chimney by ÖBB during the 1950s, all three locomotives having survived at Treibach-Althofen (499.01), Weiz (Kh 101) and Frojach (Kh 111).

Kh Class 0-10-0T no.Kh 101 was working hard at Bachl, whilst working a tourist train between Weiz and Birkfeld on 5th August 1993. *Miss S Benn*

1926 also saw the construction of three additional P Class 0-8-2Ts which were based on the three locomotives supplied to Trieste in 1911. These were initially supplied to BBÖ at St.Pölten for use on the Obergrafendorf to Gresten line. No. P 1 was destroyed during wartime service in Czechoslovakia in 1943 whilst the other two were transferred to Carinthia by the ÖBB in 1958, having become nos 199.02 and 199.03 respectively. These later 0-8-2Ts had 880mm driving wheels, 330 x 400mm cylinders, 46.4 sq.metres heating surface, 1.25 sq.metre grates and a weight of 36 tonnes. No.199.02 has been preserved in Carinthia by the *Gurktalbahn* at Treibach-Althofen whilst 199.03 is currently displayed on a plinth in Slovenia, no doubt in tribute to its earlier sisters.

StLB 0-10-0T no.Kh 101 was captured making a rousing departure from Weiz whilst hauling the same train as the previous photograph. As an example of close co-operation between the independent railways, this locomotive received a major overhaul at the Jenbach workshops of the *Zillertalbahn* in 2012.

*Miss S Benn*

The final Kh Class 0-10-0T no. Kh 111 was recorded at Mauterndorf as it prepared to depart with a train to Unzmarkt. Although intended primarily for freight duties, these powerful locomotives were often employed on passenger trains, as seen in this scene on 12th September 1958.

*D Trevor Rowe*

No.Kh 111 was viewed at Mauterndorf on the same occasion. This view shows the rear pair of driving wheels within the splayed outside frames and the Caprotti valve gear fitted to this locomotive.

*D Trevor Rowe*

No.Kh 111 was again witnessed as it attacked an incline near Ramingstein in September 1956. The Caprotti cylinders are clearly shown in this view, which were the same as those originally fitted to the Uh Class locomotives.

*P Hay*

No.Kh 111 presents a splendid sight as it storms away from Ramingstein on the same occasion, bound for Tamsweg and Mauterndorf.

*P Hay*

P Class 0-8-2T no.199.02 was recorded leaving Kühnsdorf with a freight train bound for Rechberg in Carinthia during August 1964.

*M.Grandguillaume / BVA*

Another view of the same train was obtained as no.199.02 hauled its load of standard gauge wagons mounted on "piggy-back" transporter vehicles near Sittersdorf, close to the border with Slovenia.

*M.Grandguillaume / BVA*

## Linz and Floridsdorf Steam Finale

The final and arguably finest design to emerge from Linz was introduced in 1928. These were the superheated 0-6-2Ts which were designated as the Uh Class, of which six were supplied to BBÖ followed by one to the *Zillertalbahn* in 1930. The distinction of being the final locomotive to be constructed at Linz is held by ZB no.5. Following the closure of the Linz works two further examples were built at Floridsdorf in 1931, these being the last narrow gauge locomotives constructed in Austria for use on a public railway. The eight BBÖ locomotives were distributed among various lines, where they worked alongside some of their smaller predecessors. Originally numbered Uh 01-06 (Linz) and Uh 101-102 (Floridsdorf), after 1947 they became ÖBB nos 498.01- 498.08 inclusive whilst the Jenbach based example retained its ZB identity.

These impressive machines were fitted with 800mm driving wheels, 350 x 400mm cylinders, 44.6 sq.metres of heating surface, 1.03 sq.metre grates and a weight of 28.1 tonnes. The original Linz built examples were fitted with Caprotti valve gear whilst the two later versions from Floridsdorf differed by receiving Lentz poppet valve gear. This modification to the original design proved to be very successful, the majority of the earlier variants being subsequently modified to the Lentz arrangement. One of the first locomotives to be converted was Zillertal no.5 which received its modifications in 1941, no mean achievement for a relatively small independent company to have tackled during the height of WW2!

In 1962 nos 498.01, 02 and 05 were sold to an industrial

Uh Class 0-6-2T no.498.07 was seen shunting at Waidhofen on 5th September 1958. This is one of the two locomotives built at Floridsdorf in 1931, which were fitted with Lentz Poppet Valve Gear in place of the Caprotti gear applied to the earlier Linz built examples of the Uh Class.

*D Trevor Rowe*

railway at Radmer, where they were re-gauged to 830mm in order to work at their new home until they were withdrawn from service a decade later. The remainder have all survived with 498.04 at Grünburg, 498.07 at Krimml, 498.08 (Uh 102) at Bezau and ZB5 at Jenbach. Nos 498.03 and 498.06 currently reside on plinths at Bregenz and St.Veit respectively, although the former may possibly be restored to working order at Bezau in the future. During the restoration of 498.08, the boiler and other parts of 498.03 were incorporated in the rebuilt locomotive.

The final locomotive to be constructed at Linz was this Uh Class 0-6-2T, which was dispatched to the *Zillertalbahn* and became their no.5 and subsequently named GERLOS. In this May 1985 view, the illustrious locomotive was recorded as it reversed through the yard at Jenbach prior to coupling onto the carriages seen in the background.

*J Marsh*

**Left:** Having earned its place in history as the last narrow gauge locomotive to be constructed in Austria for use on a public railway, no. Uh 102 (formerly 498.08) was displayed in its full glory when photographed at Schwarzenberg on the surviving section of the Bregenz to Bezau line, now named *Die Wälderbähnle*, on 3rd September 2006.

**Right:** Upon arrival at the upper terminus of the line at Bezau on the same occasion in September 2006, the historic locomotive was seen on the traverser at Bezau. This structure was deemed necessary to replace the former headshunt, the site of which now lies beneath the supermarket seen in the background.
*Both J F Organ*

# APPENDIX 1
## THE ORIGIN OF THE LOCOMOTIVE CLASSIFICATIONS

With the exception of the original Steyrtalbahn and SKGLB locomotives, the Austrian narrow gauge motive power was invariably identified by a class letter which referred to the depot or railway to which they were originally allocated. The principal examples were as follows:-

K – Klausen (Chiusa)
Kh – Kühnsdorf
Mh and Mv – Mariazellerbahn
P – Parenzo
T – Treibach-Althofen (in some sources Teslić)
U – Unzmarkt (StLB)
Yv – Ybbstalbahn
Z – Zell-am-See.

Logically the re-classified Bh 1 (398.01) should have retained its original Uh 1 identification, whilst the 1928 design would have been more appropriately classified as the Bh xxx series – the B referring to Bregenz where the first examples were based.

# APPENDIX 2
## PRESERVED AUSTRIAN 760 mm GAUGE LOCOMOTIVES

(All built at Linz unless stated otherwise)

Early Six Coupled Locomotives

| | |
|---|---|
| 298.102 (1888) | Grünburg |
| 298.104 (1890) | Kienberg-Gaming |
| 298.106 (1914) | Grünburg |
| SKGLB No.4 (1891) | Mondsee |
| SKGLB No.5 (1891) | Mondsee |
| SKGLB No.9 (1893) | Mondsee |
| MAR No.2 (1890) | Omaha Zoo, USA |
| StLB No.S 7 (1892) | Club 760, Frojach |
| StLB No.S 11 (1894) | Club 760, Frojach |
| StLB No.S 12 (1906) | Club 760, Frojach |
| Teslić No.DD1 (T Class 1897) | Teslić, Bosnia (Plinth) |
| StLB No. Z 6 (1893) | Club 760, Frojach |

U Class Locomotives

| | |
|---|---|
| 298.05 (1898) | Knittelfeld (Plinth) |
| 298.14 (1898) | Dorzbach (Germany) |
| 298.24 (1901) | Bezau |
| 298.25 (1901-StEG) | Bezau |
| 298.51 (1898) | Kienberg-Gaming |
| 298.52 (1898) | Grünburg |
| 298.53 (1898) | Grünburg |
| 298.54 (1898) | Ober Grafendorf |

| | |
|---|---|
| 298.55 (1899) | Kaprun, Krimml (Plinth) |
| 298.56 (1900-Flor) | Stainz (On loan from Club 760) |
| ZB 1 (1900) | Jenbach (Plinth) |
| ZB 2 (1900) | Jenbach |
| U 7 (1899) | Birkfeld |
| U 8 (1894) | Birkfeld |
| U 9 (1894) | St.Pölten (Plinth) |
| U 11 (1894) | Murau |
| U 40 (1908-Wn) | Murau |
| U 43 (1913) | Murau |
| U 44 (1922) | Birkfeld |
| U37002 (1898) | Jindřichův Hradec, Czech Republic |
| U37006 (1906) | Ružomberok, Slovakia (Plinth) |
| U37008 (1899) | Jindřichův Hradec |
| U.37 (1908-Wn) | Koper, Slovenia (Plinth) |

## Uv, Bh And Yv - U Class Derivatives

| | |
|---|---|
| 298.205 (1902) | Kienberg-Gaming |
| 298.206 (1902 | Langschlag (Plinth) |
| 298.207 (1905) | Ober Grafendorf |
| ZB 3 (1902) | Jenbach |
| Bh 1 / 398.01 (1905) | Murau |
| 598.01 (1896) | Eichgraben, Wienerwald (Plinth) |
| 598.02 / Yv2 (1896) | Waidhofen |
| 598.03 (1896) | Waidhofen |

## Spanish Locomotives (All Plinthed)

| | |
|---|---|
| SFG No.1 (1890) | San Feliu |
| SFG No.2 (1890) | Gerona |
| SFG No.6 (1905) | Llagostera (Private Collection) |
| Castellon No.5 (1890) | Borriana |
| Castellon No.7 (1890) | Gerona |

## Bosnian Linz Designed Locomotives

| | |
|---|---|
| 83-017 (1929-Bp) | Požega |
| 83-029 (1929-Bp) | Požarevac-Smederevo |
| 83-035 (1926-Jung) | Mladenovac |
| 83-037 (1929-Bp) | Požega Railway Museum |
| 83-052 (1923-Jung) | Zaječar, Šargan |
| 83-056 (1923-Jung) | Trebinje |
| 83-062 (1923-Jung) | Požega Railway Museum |
| 83-064 (1923-Jung) | Skopje |
| 83-076 (1909-Linz) | Jenbach (On loan from Club 760) |
| 83-081 (1911-Linz) | Rodoč (scrapped during civil war in 1990s) |
| 83-106 (1916-Linz) | Ploče |
| 83-157 (1948-ĐĐ) | Banovići |
| 83-173 (1949-ĐĐ) | Šargan (On loan from Požega Museum) |
| 83-175 (1949-ĐĐ) | Bijeljina |
| 83-176 (1949-ĐĐ) | Slavonski Brod |
| 83-180 (1949-ĐĐ) | Weiz-Birkfeld |
| 83-182 (1949-ĐĐ) | Lajkovac |

The only surviving Linz built example, in working order, of the numerous Bosnian 83 Class 0-8-2s is no.83-076. This historic machine now operates in its country of birth at the *Zillertalbahn*, where it carries the number ZB4. It is viewed at Jenbach in June 1998.                                                                    *G Brown*

Note: The majority of the class 83 locomotives are either in museums or displayed on plinths. The only definitely known working examples are nos 83-052, 83-076, 83-157, 83-173 and 83-180.

| | |
|---|---|
| 73-002 (1907-Linz) | Požega Railway Museum |
| 73-018 (1913-Bp) | Jablanica |
| 73-019 (1913-Bp) | Zell-Am-See |
| | (On loan from Club 760) |

Note: Only 73-019 Is In Working Order.

## Mh Class Locomotives

| | |
|---|---|
| 399.01 (1906) | Gmünd |
| 399.02 (1906) | Gmünd |
| 399.03 / Mh 3 (1906) | Zell-Am-See |
| 399.04 (1906) | Gmünd |
| 399.05 (1908) | Grünburg |
| 399.06 / Mh 6 (1908) | Ober Grafendorf |

## K Class Locomotive

| | |
|---|---|
| R410.005 (1916) | Plan, Italy (Plinth) |

## Kh Class Locomotives

| | |
|---|---|
| 499.01 (1924) | Treibach-Althofen |
| Kh 101 (1926) | Weiz-Birkfeld |
| Kh 111 (1930) | Club 760, Frojach |

## P Class Locomotives

| | |
|---|---|
| 199.02 (1926) | Treibach-Althofen |
| 199.03 (1926) | Isola, Slovenia (Plinth) |

## Uh Class Locomotives

| | |
|---|---|
| 498.03 (1929) | Bregenz (Plinth) |
| 498.04 (1929) | Grünburg |
| 498.06 (1930) | St. Veit (Plinth) |
| 498.07 (1931-Flor) | Krimml |
| 498.08 / Uh 102 (1931-Flor) | Bezau |
| ZB 5 (1930) | Jenbach |